Family Reunion

To my family—
Here's to our reunions,
those in the past,
those to come!
—M.Q.

I wish to extend a heartfelt thank you to the D.C. Commission
on the Arts and Humanities, under the National Endowment
for the Arts, for a creative writing grant during the time these
poems were written. I also wish to acknowledge and thank
Cricket magazine, which first published "Sunday Morning" in a
slightly different form.
                                                              —M.Q.

Text © 2004 by Mary Quattlebaum
Illustrations © 2004 by Andrea Shine
Published 2004 by Eerdmans Books for Young Readers
An imprint of Wm. B. Eerdmans Publishing Company
255 Jefferson S.E., Grand Rapids, Michigan 49503
P.O. Box 163, Cambridge CB3 9PU U.K.

04 05 06 07 08 09 7 6 5 4 3 2 1

ISBN 0-8028-5237-8

The illustrations were created with watercolor and cut paper.
The display type was set in Cantoria.
Art Director—Gayle Brown
Graphic Designer—Matthew Van Zomeren

Family Reunion

Written by Mary Quattlebaum   Illustrated by Andrea Shine

Phone Call from Nana

Hi, Jodie! How are you?
'Round here not much is new
except the trees now wear
their best bright green and share
their twigs with baby things,
all chirpy-soft. Night brings
us heaps of starry blue
and we are missing you.
Can you visit soon?
Let's plan a week in June!

Getting There

One last good-bye; we're on the road,
which stretches like a thin, black thread
so far before our creeping load.

Sigh! So many miles ahead!
Miles and miles of cars, trees, signs;
of sipping soda, sweet and red;

of coloring—*bump!*—outside the lines;
of asking, "Are we almost there?"
Dad groans, "Please, no more sighs or whines."

"All right," I sigh, "then you won't care
that Matt's gone greener than his cap."
We stop so Matt can gulp some air,

then strap him close to Mama's lap.
And as he sleeps the shadows grow
all thick and black. I clutch the map

and think of folks I barely know
coming far fast, coming sleek
and slow from places I don't know. . . .

"We're here," Dad shouts. I shyly peek.
Mama kisses someone's cheek.
What will we do for one whole week?

Antique Rocker

I remember this chair:
smooth, curved back, the hug
of oak arms, the wood's whirl
unique as a fingerprint.
   Rock-rock, rock-rock.

This chair has rocked since 1884.
Rocked from child to child,
through children, grandchildren, more and more.
Two years ago it fit just right.
   Rock-rock, rock-rock.

And now it's tight.
So small! This chair never grew.
It never left. Day after day, it holds
the touch of forgotten hands.
   Rock-rock, rock-rock.

It holds me, too.
I watch the sky fill
with countless stars, listen
to the house's sleeping breath.
   Rock-rock, rock-rock, rock-rock.

Shag's Greeting

First to rise,
Shag gives my nose
a pink-tongued "hi,"
then off he goes

with a doggy grin,
licking each chin,
tugging each sheet,
leading us in

like sleepy sheep.
We sniff . . . and wake!
Grandpa flips
the first pancake.

And as we eat,
Shag brings my shoes,
yawns three times—
and takes a snooze.

Cloud Visions

The clouds today are big as dreams,
fancy dancing free and high.
Hank sees a guitar. Hear the beat?
We clap as it goes strumming by.

Matt spies a pie piled high with cream.
Grandpa spots a puffy throne.
Baby points to four fat chicks
while Shag barks at a floating bone.

I wave—and wonder what clouds see
looking down and watching me.

Baby's Favorite Game

Tackle game, tickle game,
grab your leg and giggle game.

Flouncing game, pouncing game,
climbing backs and bouncing game.

Here comes Baby! She won't miss
when she tags you with a kiss.

Watermelon

Melon, melon, green and round,
fat with fruit, all red and sweet.
Thump! We make a ripe, drum sound.

We heave the melon off the ground,
slice the rind and start to eat
melon, melon, green and round.

We spit out each small seed that's found
sliding through our cool-juice treat,
then thump our tummies—what a sound!

Hank sprays the hose and droplets bound
down arms and legs, and chase from feet
all trace of melon, green and round,

'til all that's left in one big mound
are rinds and seeds in summer heat.
The sun beats down without a sound.

We pat one seed into the ground
made damp with water, cool and sweet.
Melon, melon, green and round,
next summer—*thump!*—that ripe, drum sound.

Grandpa's Maple Tree

Stiff, earth-stuck, strong,
it trembles when touched
by bird-wing or breeze.
Silent, it welcomes song.

Hard, it shelters heart-
wood and pith while gently
taking sun and rain.
Breathing, it gives us breath.

Harsh winter strips it bare.
Spring turns it green.
This tree is big
yet once it fit

inside a maple seed.

Hank's Dad

He's a voice on the phone now.
He's a voice once a week
saying, "How's the big guy?"

He's a name on a postcard.
He's a name on a package
with a red birthday bow.

He's a note gone sad,
a dad far off, a face
on paper in a secret place.

So when folks say,
"Hank's got his daddy's blue-
blue eyes and tuneful way,"

Hank must dig down deep
to find that face.
Dad's been gone so long.

Hank's Glass Harp

Twenty empty goblets; four neat rows.
Hank measures water out in careful drips.
The audience grows bored. Shag starts to doze.
With shirt sleeves rolled, the maestro slowly dips
long fingers in each quiet, half-filled glass
and lightly taps to tune those common things.
Then suddenly he gives a quick palm-pass
across one rim and—*ting!*—the first note rings
out brief and crystalline and—*ting!*—floats high
above the roof, above the trees—*ting! ting!*—
above the birds—*ting! ting!*—into the sky . . .
to shimmer bright as angel wings. *Ting!*
The last note softly holds . . . then dies. A pause.
Hank shyly bows. The air brims with applause.

A Feast and Talk-Fest

Grandpa grills and stacks the burgers,
I place them on each bun.
Uncle adds his special sauce
and sneaks a bite of one.

Aunts are chatting in the garden
while choosing beans with care.
Matt snaps some with karate chops
and strings one in my hair.

Hank whistles salad into bowls,
Matt empties out a bag.
Baby's corn becomes a cob
thrown high and far for Shag.

Then plates are gently pushed aside.
The sun starts sitting low
as grown folks settle in their chairs
and stories start to flow:

The one about the mighty fish
that pulled aunt in the lake,
the time poor uncle burned the roof
baking birthday cake.

How Mama saved a wounded duck
and Nana lost her cool
when aunt played that joke on what's-his-name,
the bully down at school.

Above, the first stars blink, surprised
to hear all that they did.
How . . . how *strange* to see in these old tales
each grown-up as a kid.

Lightning Bugs

Night has swallowed earth
and sky. Oh, look! Moon showers
us with crumbs of light.

Sunday Morning

Nana moves
through the room
like a teeny
splash of sea, croons
bread into toast,
hums water
into tea. But we know
come church time, she
will rise in blue
with the choir, Alleluia,
and their sound like waves
gonna roll,
gonna roll,
gonna roll out deep and wondrous, strong,
growing that song into sea-roar. Alleluia!

Going Back

One last, big hug—we're on our way,
and I watch my family wave and smile,
grow smaller . . . smaller . . . far, far away,

as we travel back, mile after mile.
We whine and color, sip and sigh,
pass trees and signs and one huge pile

of honking cars. The miles slip by.
And I slip into sleep and dream
and, dreaming, watch my family fly

under cloud and over stream
to places that I'd like to see:
Baby's beach washed blue and cream,

the fussy gulls above the sea,
and fog that cottons everything.
I want to hear the harmony

of desert winds that softly sing
to sands as still as hot, dry snow,
which rise, Hank says, and dancing bring—

"Home," Dad sighs. And I walk slow
and silent through the door, then go
straight to my bedroom's small, welcome glow.

Letter to Nana

Hello,
Hope you are fine.
Our trip was long—just sign,
tree, sign the whole way back.
And now my window's black
with sudden rain, and the cars
wink dull as fallen stars—
but our family week shines bright
in my mind. . . . Is it all right
to start the plans this soon
to meet again next June?

        Love,
        Jodie